Let's look at
EYES

First published in 2003 by Zero To Ten Limited
327 High Street, Slough, Berkshire, SL1 1TX
and 814 North Franklin Street, Chicago, Illinois 60610
This edition published under license from Zero To Ten Limited.
All rights reserved.

Copyright © 2003 Zero To Ten Limited
Text copyright © 2003 Simona Sideri
Illustrations copyright © 2003 Sheilagh Noble

Publisher: Anna McQuinn, Art director: Tim Foster, Publishing assistant:
Vikram Parashar

Published in the United States by Smart Apple Media
1980 Lookout Drive, North Mankato, Minnesota 56003

U.S. publication copyright © 2005 Smart Apple Media
International copyright reserved in all countries. No part of this book may
be reproduced in any form without written permission from the publisher.
Printed in China

Library of Congress Cataloging-in-Publication Data

Sideri, Simona.
Eyes / written by Simona Sideri ; illustrated by Sheilagh Noble.
p. cm. — (Let's look at)
Summary: Young children describe the eyes of different animals.
ISBN 1-58340-495-3
1. Eye—Juvenile literature. 2. Vision—Juvenile literature. [1. Eye. 2. Animals.] I. Noble,
Sheilagh, ill. II. Title. III. Let's look at (North Mankato, Minn.)

QP475.7.S536 2004
573.8'8—dc22   2003058959

9 8 7 6 5 4 3 2 1

Let's look at
EYES

Written by
Simona Sideri

Illustrated by
Sheilagh Noble

Look at me. I use my eyes to see!

Eagles have excellent eyes!
They can spot their prey
from high in the sky.

Camels have bushy brows that shade their eyes from the desert sun.

They also have long eyelashes to keep out flying sand.

Owls don't move
their eyes, so they
always look like
they're staring.

Instead, they turn their heads to see in all directions!

Bush babies can see in the dark.

They are good night hunters.

Lobsters' eyes are on the end of little stalks. They can peek out from behind rocks to check for danger.

Wasps have amazing eyes
made up of many parts.

Each part of the eye
sees just a small part
of whatever they are looking at!

Eyes are excellent!